Backyard
SCIENTIST

BACKYARD
METEOROLOGY
EXPERIMENTS

Alix Wood

PowerKiDS
press

New York

Published in 2019 by Rosen Publishing
29 East 21st Street, New York, NY 10010

Produced for Rosen Publishing by Alix Wood Books
Designed by Alix Wood
Editor: Eloise Macgregor
Projects devised and photographed by Kevin Wood

Photo credits:
Cover, 1, 6 left, 10 left, 17 background, 20, 24 background © Adobe Stock Images;
4 bottom © USGS; all other photos © Kevin Wood

Cataloging-in-Publication Data
Names: Wood, Alix.
Title: Backyard meteorology experiments / Alix Wood.
Description: New York : PowerKids Press, 2019. | Series: Backyard scientist | Includes glossary and index.
Identifiers: LCCN ISBN 9781538337424 (pbk.) | ISBN 9781538337417 (library bound) | ISBN 9781538337431 (6 pack)
Subjects: LCSH: Meteorology--Experiments--Juvenile literature. | Weather--Experiments--Juvenile literature.
Classification: LCC QC981.3 W64 2019 | DDC 551.5078--dc23

Printed in the United States of America

CPSIA compliance information: Batch # CS18PK: For further information contact Rosen Publishing, New York, New York at 1-800-237-9932.

Contents

What Is Meteorology?

Meteorology is the study of changes in the weather. Have you ever wondered how weather forecasters know what the weather will be like? Meteorologists use all different kinds of tools to forecast whether it will rain, snow, or thunder, and whether it will be hot or cold.

WEATHER FORECAST

SAT	SUN
77°	69°	70
65°	58°	62

Studying the Weather

It can be important to know what the weather will be like, especially in **extreme** places, like the top of a mountain. Meteorologists use tools to measure things such as the speed of the wind, and how much rainfall there has been. They measure the **air pressure** to figure out what the weather will be like over the next few days. You can make all these weather-predicting tools in this book. Try it, and become a weather expert!

Setting Up Your Backyard Laboratory

Find an outside space that you can use to do these experiments. Some of them can be messy! Remember to check with whomever owns the space that it is OK to do your experiments there. You may want to find a picnic table to work on.

You should be able to find most of the things you will need around your home or yard. You may need to buy some small items, so check the "You Will Need" section before you start a project.

BE SCIENTIFIC

As a scientist, it is important to be precise. It is not always easy to forecast the weather. Forecasters would rather say the weather will be unpredictable than guess incorrectly. Knowing what the weather will be like is really important to people in jobs such as agriculture, transportation, and fishing. The wrong forecast can even put lives in danger!

STAYING SAFE

Science experiments can be dangerous. The experiments in this book have been specially chosen because they are fun and relatively safe, but you must still be careful. Ask an adult to help you. Follow all warnings. Wear any suggested protective clothing, and be careful.

Make a Barometer

One of the best tools for predicting changes in the weather is a **barometer**. A barometer measures the pressure in the air. Changes in air pressure affect our weather. High pressure usually means we will get clear weather, and low pressure means we are likely to get unsettled, stormy weather.

Barometers like this one have a small flexible box inside. Small changes in air pressure cause the box to expand or contract, which moves the needle around the dial.

YOU WILL NEED:

- jar or coffee tin
- balloon
- rubber band
- PVA glue
- straw
- card stock and a cereal box
- markers

Try making your own barometer.

1 Stretch a piece of balloon over the glass jar or coffee tin. Put a rubber band around it to secure it in place. Make sure the tin or jar is airtight.

2

Place a straw so one end is at the center of the jar, and the other end sticks out over the edge. Glue it in place.

3

Glue a sheet of card stock to a cereal box. Stand it next to your barometer. Draw the sun just above the top of the lid, and a cloud just below the lid.

WHAT'S HAPPENING?

When air pressure is high, air is pressing down on the balloon, causing the straw to point up. When air pressure is low, the air in the jar pushes up against the balloon, causing the straw to point down.

4

Mark where the top of the straw points with a line, and note the time. Did the air pressure change during the day?

— 10 a.m.

Measuring Wind Speed

Air travels from areas of high pressure to areas of low pressure. This movement creates wind. Wind speed can be measured using a tool known as an **anemometer**. Here's how you can make your own.

1 Ask an adult to help you poke four evenly spaced holes around the sides of one cup, using scissors. Make another hole in the middle of the bottom of the cup.

2 Push the straws through the holes so they overlap in the center of the cup.

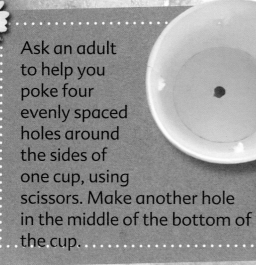

3 Make two holes opposite each other in the other four cups.

8

4

Thread the four cups onto the straws, as shown, so the top of one cup faces the bottom of the one in front.

5

Insert the pencil, eraser first, up through the hole in the center cup. Poke a pin through the two straws and into the eraser.

Your anemometer will spin around in the wind. Marking one cup will help you count the spins more easily.

WHAT'S HAPPENING?

Air is made up of tiny **molecules.** The molecules in the wind hit the anemometer and cause it to spin. See how windy it is each day by comparing how many times the anemometer spins in one minute.

9

Make a Simple Sundial

Long ago, people used the shadows cast by the sun to tell the time. A sundial shows the time of day by the position of the shadow made by a pointer. Sundials can be amazingly accurate, and are really simple to make. Try making one yourself.

1

Find a sunny place outdoors. You want your sundial to be in the open, away from anything that may put it in a shadow.

2

Push your stick into the soil. If your open space is paved, put the stick in a flowerpot filled with soil, to help hold it upright on the hard surface.

3

Write each daylight hour's number on a rock, using paint or a marker.

4

At every hour of daylight, place its numbered rock where the shadow falls, around 1 foot (30 cm) from the base of the stick.

WHAT'S HAPPENING?

The Earth spins as it travels in space. This makes the Sun appear to move in the sky. The shadow the Sun casts as its position changes is so regular it can help us keep time.

5

Now your sundial is ready to use. The Sun's shadow will point to the correct time.

Tornado in a Bottle!

A **tornado** is a powerful, funnel-shaped wind that touches the ground. Violent tornadoes can travel at up to 300 miles (483 km) per hour. They form from storm clouds created by moist air. When the cloud meets cold, dry air it can start to spin sideways. Rising air then tilts the rotating air **vertically**, forming a tornado. Try making this spinning tornado in a bottle.

YOU WILL NEED:

- 2 large, clear plastic bottles
- water
- duct tape
- food coloring
- glitter

1

Fill one plastic bottle 2/3 full of water. Add a couple of drops of food coloring and a sprinkle of glitter.

2

Place the second bottle upside down on top of the first. Tape the two bottles' necks tightly together using duct tape.

3 Turn your tornado-maker upside down, so that the bottle with water is on the top.

4 Quickly swirl the bottle in a circular motion.

5 You should start to see a swirling tornado form inside your bottle!

WHAT'S HAPPENING?

As the spinning water rushes into the bottom bottle, it creates a swirling **vortex**, similar to a tornado. The glitter acts like flying **debris** would in a real tornado, getting caught up in the swirling action.

A Cloud in a Jar

A cloud is formed when **water vapor** in the air **condenses** into water droplets. The droplets attach to tiny **particles** in the air and form a cloud. Try creating your own cloud with this cool experiment.

1

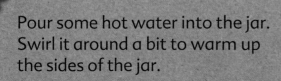

First, place the jar lid in the freezer for about 15 minutes. Put some ice cubes in a bag and secure them to the top of the lid using the rubber band.

2

Pour some hot water into the jar. Swirl it around a bit to warm up the sides of the jar.

14

3

Quickly spray some hair spray into the jar. Put on the lid with the ice still on top.

4

You should see some **condensation** start to form above the water. Take off the lid and let your "cloud" go!

WHAT'S HAPPENING?

When you put warm water in the jar, some of the water turns into vapor, and rises to the top of the jar. When it reaches the cold lid, the water vapor cools down and condenses. A cloud will only form if there are particles for it to condense on to. The hair spray **mimics** dust particles, and helps form the cloud.

Make Some Lightning

Try making your own lightning. Warning! This experiment gives you a tiny electric shock. Unlike real lightning, the shock is just **static electricity** though, so it won't harm you. To see your lightning at its best, do this experiment outside at night. The spark of electricity is easier to see in the dark.

YOU WILL NEED:

- aluminum pie pan
- some wool fabric
- a styrofoam plate (ours was from under a frozen pizza)
- a pencil with a new eraser
- a thumbtack

1 Push a thumbtack up through the center of the pie pan. Push the eraser end of the pencil into the thumbtack.

2 Put the styrofoam plate on a table. Rub the plate vigorously with the wool for a couple of minutes.

3 Quickly pick up the aluminum pie pan using the pencil. Place it on top of the styrofoam plate.

WHAT'S HAPPENING?

Real lightning can be dangerous, so it is best to stay indoors in a storm. Lightning is a bright flash of electricity produced by a thunderstorm. Lightning happens when **negative charges** in the bottom of a storm cloud are attracted to **positive charges** in the ground. In this experiment, rubbing the styrofoam with wool charges your pie dish. When you touch the pie dish, that charge leaps from the dish to your finger, creating a spark!

4 Pick up the pie pan again. Touch the aluminum with your finger. You should feel a tiny shock and see a spark!

17

Measuring Rainfall

Meteorologists often talk about how many inches or centimeters of rainfall have fallen over a certain period of time. It is interesting to compare how much rain falls in your neighborhood week after week. You can measure your local rainfall yourself by making this simple rain **gauge**.

1

Draw a line around the middle of the plastic bottle using a marker. Ask an adult to help you cut the bottle in half along the line.

2

At the point before the bottle starts to curve inward at the base, draw a line around the bottom of the bottle.

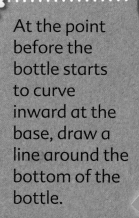

Decide if you want to measure the rainfall in inches or centimeters. Using a ruler and marker, draw a scale on the bottle, starting from your drawn line.

3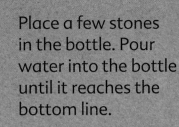

Place a few stones in the bottle. Pour water into the bottle until it reaches the bottom line.

4

Turn the top upside down and tape it to the bottle.

5

Put your rain gauge outside in the open. After any rainfall, check to see how far up the scale the water has risen.

WHAT'S HAPPENING?

Your rain gauge shows how much rain fell on the exact spot you placed your bottle. After a day of heavy rain, the water level might rise 1 inch (2.5 cm). This means that 1 inch (2.5 cm) of rain fell on the ground in that spot.

Making Rainbows

Did you know that visible light is made up of the seven different colors that you see in a rainbow? Rainbows appear during wet, sunny weather. The water droplets split the light into its seven colors. Try making your own rainbow. Be careful where you spray your water, and be prepared to get wet!

YOU WILL NEED:

- a hose or spray bottle
- a CD
- a sheet of white paper
- a flashlight (if it is cloudy)
- white card stock
- markers
- a skewer

1 On a sunny day, stand in an open spot. Create a mist using a hose with a spray attachment, or a spray bottle. Be careful where you spray it!

2 If you stand between the sun and the mist you should be able to see a rainbow! Can you see the seven colors?

3

Hold a CD in the sunshine, or if it's cloudy, shine a flashlight at it. You should see the seven colors that make up the rainbow.

4

Hold the CD so light reflecting off it shines onto some white paper. You should see a rainbow appear.

WHAT'S HAPPENING?

Just as raindrops split white light into a rainbow, white light can be made by mixing those seven colors together. Try it yourself. Draw the color wheel on the right onto some card stock using markers. Cut out your circle. Pierce the center with a skewer, so it is like a spinning top. Quickly spin the wheel. What color do you see?

Create Rain in a Bag

Did you know that Earth has been recycling the same water for billions of years? Heat from the Sun causes water to **evaporate** and rise into the sky. The water vapor gets cold and forms clouds. This is called condensation. The clouds get heavy and water falls back to Earth as rain, hail, sleet, or snow. Then the whole cycle can start again.

YOU WILL NEED:

- small ziplock bag
- 1/4 cup of water
- blue food coloring
- tape
- markers

1 Using markers, draw a sun, cloud, and the ocean onto the bag.

2 Pour 1/4 cup of water into the ziplock bag.

3

Add a little blue food coloring.

4

Seal the ziplock bag shut.

WHAT'S HAPPENING?

The water in your bag gets warm in the sunlight, and some evaporates. As the water vapor cools at the top of the bag, condensation will form like a cloud. When the air can't hold any more condensation, the water falls down as rain.

5 Tape the bag to the inside of a sunny window. Soon, condensation will start to form, and your cloud will begin to "rain!"

Make a Thermometer

A thermometer measures how hot or cold something is. A thermometer's glass tube contains a liquid, such as mercury or alcohol, which **expands** when it is hot and **contracts** when it gets cold. A written scale then tells you the temperature. Try making your own thermometer.

YOU WILL NEED:

- small clear plastic bottle
- water
- rubbing alcohol
- clear plastic drinking straw
- modeling clay
- food coloring

1

Fill the bottle a quarter full with equal parts of water and rubbing alcohol.

Add a few drops of food coloring to the mixture.

24

Put the straw in the bottle. Don't let it go all the way to the bottom. Use modeling clay to seal the neck of the bottle, to keep the straw in place. You want the straw to be under the liquid, but not to touch the bottom of the bottle.

Warm your thermometer by holding your hands on the bottom of the bottle. Watch the mixture move up through the straw, showing the temperature rise.

WHAT'S HAPPENING?

Your thermometer works just like any other thermometer. The mixture expands when warmed. As the bottle is full of liquid and air, the expanding mixture has nowhere else to go, except to travel up the straw. If the temperature was very hot, the mixture would come out of the top of the straw!

Weather Forecasting

See if you can forecast the weather for tomorrow. Use the barometer you made to see if the weather will be stormy or not. Check the wind speed with your anemometer. Can you tell if the wind is coming from a hot or cold place? Then you can make your prediction using this weather chart. Turn the dial to choose a prediction, and then check if you were right in the morning!

1

Place a plate on your sheet of card stock. Draw around the plate using a pencil.

2

Find the center of your circle. Using a ruler, divide the circle into eight equal segments.

3

Draw a picture in each segment showing all the different types of weather you might get.

WHAT'S HAPPENING?

Weather forecasting predictions are based on science. Barometers and anemometers help forecasters predict approaching weather. Meteorologists also use **satellite** images to track weather as it moves around the world.

4

Cut out your weather predictor and place it on a larger piece of thick card. Push a thumbtack through the center. Write "Tomorrow's Forecast" at the top of your spinner. Now you can select your weather prediction by turning the spinner.

Tomorrow's Forecast

Are you a meteorology genius? Test yourself with these questions. The answers are on page 29.

1. What does a barometer measure?
a) changes in wind direction
b) how high a cloud is
c) changes in air pressure

2. What instrument do meteorologists use to measure wind speed?
a) a ruler b) an anemometer c) a thermometer

3. Air traveling from areas of high pressure to areas of low pressure causes what type of weather?
a) wind b) snow c) sunshine

4. High pressure usually means we will get unsettled weather.
a) true b) false

5. You can tell the time by looking at the shadows made by the Sun
a) true b) false

6. A really strong tornado can travel at what speed?

a) up to 300 miles (483 km) per hour
b) up to 30 miles (48.3 km) per hour
c) up to 3 miles (4.83 km) per hour

7. Lightning is a flash of electricity.

a) true b) false

8. What does a rain gauge measure?

a) whether it is likely to rain
b) how much rain fell in one spot
c) how waterproof your umbrella is

9. The water you drink out of your faucet is actually billions of years old.

a) true b) false

10. What does a thermometer measure?

a) air pressure b) rainfall c) temperature

Answers

1. c) changes in air pressure; 2. b) an anemometer; 3. a) wind;
4. b) false; 5. a) true; 6. a) up to 300 miles (483 km) per hour;
7. a) true; 8. b) how much rain fell in one spot; 9. a) true;
10. c) temperature

Glossary

air pressure The force exerted by the weight of the air.

anemometer An instrument for measuring wind speed.

barometer An instrument that measures the pressure of the atmosphere.

condensation Water which collects as droplets on a cold surface.

condenses Changes from a gas or vapor to a liquid.

contracts Becomes smaller.

debris The remains of something.

evaporate Turning into vapor from a liquid state.

expands To increase in size.

extreme Far from the ordinary or average.

gauge A measuring instrument.

mimics Imitates.

molecules The smallest particle of a substance.

negative charges Having more electrons than protons.

particles Very small parts of matter (such as molecules).

positive charges Having less electrons than protons.

satellite A man-made object intended to orbit Earth, or another celestial body.

static electricity A stationary electric charge, typically produced by friction.

tornado A violent destructive whirling wind accompanied by a funnel-shaped cloud.

vertically Going straight up or down from a level surface.

vortex A mass of whirling fluid forming a cavity in the center toward which things are drawn.

water vapor Water in a gaseous form.

For More Information

Mullins, Matt. *Think Like a Scientist in the Backyard*. Ann Arbor, MI: Cherry Lake Publishing, 2012.

Riechmann, Annie, and Dawn Suzette Smith. *Whatever the Weather: Science Experiments and Art Activities That Explore the Wonders of Weather*. Boulder, CO: Roost Books, 2016.

Taylor-Butler, Christine. *Meteorology: The Study of Weather*. New York, NY: Children's Press, 2012.

Wilder, Nellie. *Changing Weather*. Huntington Beach, CA: Teacher Created Materials, 2015.

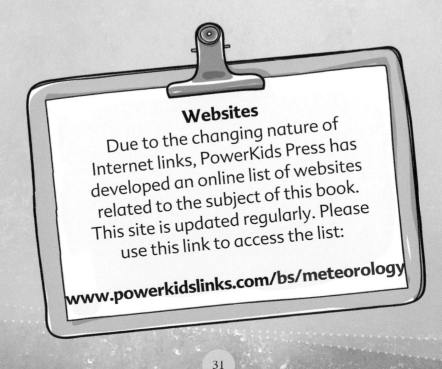

Websites
Due to the changing nature of Internet links, PowerKids Press has developed an online list of websites related to the subject of this book. This site is updated regularly. Please use this link to access the list:

www.powerkidslinks.com/bs/meteorology

Index